FROM WHERE I'M STANDING

"This is what the view looks like from my vantage point!"

Marilyn Avient

From Where I'am Standing

Marilyn Avient

© Marilyn Avient 2007

Published by 1stWorld Publishing
1100 North 4th St. Fairfield, Iowa 52556
tel: 641-209-5000 • fax: 641-209-3001
web: www.1stworldpublishing.com

LCCN: 2007929041

SoftCover ISBN: 978-1-4218-9970-1

All rights reserved. No part of this book may be reproduced or utilized in any form or by any means, electronic or mechanical, including photocopying or recording, or by any information storage and retrieval system, without permission in writing from the author.

This material has been written and published solely for educational purposes. The author and the publisher shall have neither liability or responsibility to any person or entity with respect to any loss, damage or injury caused or alleged to be caused directly or indirectly by the information contained in this book.

I DEDICATE THIS BOOK

to

Irene Martina

for her love, encouragement, and confidence,
in everything I do.
At her urging, I wrote this workbook in 2003.

ACKNOWLEDGEMENTS

John,
you are a part of everything I do.
What would I do without you?

Thank you

to

all the good people at

1st World Publishing!

It's been fun!

WELCOME TO MY WORLD!

Life really is much simpler than many of us choose to make it-the operative word being "choose." The fact that I can and do choose each detail of my life is empowering to me because that puts me in charge. Everything that happens to me has been chosen by me on a soul level to provide the learning I need for spiritual growth. I have chosen every person who crosses my path because of the lessons that he or she will give to me for my soul's advancement. Many people find this to be a heavy concept, but to me, from my vantage point, I really do feel **enlighten-ed** by it.

I have spent my life looking deeper into myself than most people care to look. The pay-off is that I feel stronger, more powerful, and more peaceful than I ever thought possible when I started out on this quest to find my truth. Life is one big choice that begins at the moment I wake up every morning when I have to choose between smiling or frowning as my first act of the day.

By accepting this concept of *"choice,"* the possibility of being a victim is eliminated. I spent half a century feeling afraid of anything and everything, and I felt as though I were a victim to life itself. I was angry that I seemed to be the only person in the world who lived that way. Now I know that it's ok to be afraid. Rather than being at the mercy of the fear, I know that I may choose NOT to have it and, therefore, it loses all of its power. That one concept alone was enough to set me free without looking at any other issues—but I looked at them anyway.

Many wonderful discussions came out of these topics when I wrote them for a group that I belonged to in Edmonton, Alberta. It did not take too much encouragement for me to decide to put them into this book for others, such as yourself, to enjoy.

There are no right or wrong answers for any of the questions because they are to be answered *from where you are standing*. Your answers will reflect life as you see it from your vantage point. This process will no doubt be a serious aid in your journey, but it is also meant to be fun. I have often chosen to take life very seriously in the past, but now, *from where I am standing*, I am indeed beginning to see the lightness and the joy that exists everywhere. No matter how ominous a situation appears to be on the surface I just have to *choose* to see it differently!

Enjoy! Happy journeying!

Peace be with you,

Marilyn Avient

I would suggest that you make a contract with yourself promising that you will do your very best to do these exercises with honesty and complete willingness to let yourself *feel*. Remember; it is impossible ... yourself.

My Contract with Myself

I, _____, willingly make the following contract with myself, and do hereby swear to uphold the promises declared herein.

I, _____, promise myself the following:

_____   _____
Signed   Date

ACCOUNTABILITY

A-C-C-O-U-N-T-A-B-I-L-I-T-Y That is how the dictionary says it is spelled, but I prefer to spell it P-O-W-E-R. I have lived in fear for most of my life and have always felt that I was incapable of changing that. The big and all consuming fear was slowly and methodically suffocating me—I became claustrophobic as the blackness pushed me further and further into a corner! I hated my life and I hated my cowardice! One day, after I had spent long years going in and out of psych wards due to severe depression, I was handed a book called Happiness Is a Choice. I was so insulted that this person thought I needed this book that I threw it across the room and said that only a fool would choose to be this unhappy. I, then, stubbornly resumed my victim stance.

I may have outwardly discarded the book with the offensive title, but I did not forget it. I wanted to completely disprove that title; instead, I only succeeded in proving it to be correct. Through my own investigations—therapists, books, soul-searching, seminars, and much more—I amazingly discovered that *I…yes…I* was in charge and in control of everything that happened in my life. All of a sudden, I knew what it would feel like to win the lottery! I discovered for myself that happiness (and every other emotion) really is a choice and, up until then, I had not chosen well.

Once this realization was firmly in place, I knew that I could fly! This does not mean that I chose to be happy every day after that; it means that I knew that no matter what happened in my day I was responsible. **What** we choose is not as important as knowing that we are directly or indirectly accountable for everything that happens to us. By choosing to be resentful and angry for many years of our lives, we may have to realize one day that we have also chosen to have cancer or some other fatal disease, which are so often the direct result of those all-consuming emotions that literally eat us up inside. We choose the way we want people to treat us by the energy that we give off and by the attitudes we display.

Accountability is a dreaded topic for many, because it is so much easier to be at the mercy of the outside world and to be able to blame something (or someone) else for the challenges we find before us every day. I do not understand that way of thinking because it makes me feel so hopeless, so desperate, and so out of control. I feel great strength when I look at a day that I am enjoying and realize that I created it with my attitudes, my beliefs, and my faith. I feel even stronger when I look at a day that is filled with sadness, depression, and other troubles, because I realize that if I created these feelings, then I can change them. On those days, I give myself permission to feel what I am feeling, but I put a time limit on it.

All events that happen outside of us are neutral and, standing on their own, they have no clout at all. Our reactions to these external incidents are what make the events personal to us; that is the part over which we have total control and for which we are entirely accountable. The event itself requires no particular response, but our history around that event and our former responses make us think there is only one correct way to react. For instance, the phone rings. I answer it. Is that a necessity? Is there any other possible response? Does the ringing phone *expect* any particular reaction?

Accountability = Responsibility

Responsibility = Response-ability = Ability to Respond

Questions

1. What are your thoughts about accountability?

2. Give an example of a response to a particular event in your life that you could improve upon.

3. Rewrite the example in #2 and change your response to something that would please you.

4. Name some societal events that always get the same responses from people in general. Are the traditional responses the only possible ones? Discuss in writing.

5. Have a fun day responding to neutral events in the opposite way that you do now? For example if you usually swear at drivers who cut you off in traffic, try smiling and waving.

AFFIRMATIONS

Affirmations are useful tools for changing the negative self-talk that goes on in each of us. Picture yourself as a computer, with your brain being the hard-drive, and all that you have been taught being the data stored within your many files and folders. This data includes all of our information—the good and the not so good, most of which came to us as children when we were desperately seeking clues to our identity. If someone tells you "You're a bad boy!" often enough, then it becomes knowledge that you believe to be true, and so you store it in your "hard-drive" as such. This is the information that we use to guide us through life!

When I was growing up, my friend's little brother honestly thought that his name was "Bad Boy." Almost every day, this poor little guy was called that by some member of his family; usually his mother. If anyone were to ask him what his name was, he would say, "Bad Boy!" without any hesitation at all.

Examples of information that we have all stored to one degree or another:

✦ "Life is a struggle."

✦ "Don't worry; you'll just have to work a little harder than most."

✦ "Money is the root of all evil."

✦ "A person like you should just be grateful for what you've got."

✦ "You are over-emotional and too sensitive. They're going to eat you alive!"

✦ "You are a very hard-to-love child."

✦ "You have to be careful—the world is just waiting for you to let down your guard."

✦ "You're a very homely girl, but somewhere there will be a man who won't mind!"

ETC! ETC! ETC! ETC!

These are messages that are given to us as children, and we store them away in our "computer hard-drives." We play them over and over in our heads, and whenever we are in applicable situations, we pull them out and live them as though they were fact. We all have thousands of these statements in us. That is the bad news.

The good news is that if we put these words *into* our "computer", we can also *take them out*. One method is to push the DELETE key, but human computers do not like empty space, so this method is effective, but only temporarily. The best way is to replace the space occupied by the old files with new and affirmative statements as soon as the DELETE key is pushed.

An affirmation is a positive statement that we desire to be true about ourselves. It is always stated in the present tense in words that feel comfortable for us to say. Negative terms are to be absolutely avoided. We make each statement as though it is true right now.

For example, an affirmation is NOT the following:

- "I am not an unlovable person."
- "I will not be afraid any more."

Examples of good affirmations:

- "I deserve to have good and wonderful things happen to me."
- "I am lovable."
- "I am successful and well-respected."
- "One by one, I am overcoming all of my fears."
- "I am beautiful."
- "I am a creative, powerful, and trustworthy woman."
- "I am speaking to crowds in conference halls all over the world."

Affirmations can be fun and they serve a very valuable purpose. They tell you the things that you have been longing to hear all of your life. The more you tell yourself something, the more you will believe it to be true. And, one day, it will be.

MORE ON "AFFIRMATIONS"

And now that you have acquainted yourself with the concept of affirmations, let us go a little deeper with them. In the first section, we talked about the effect of affirmations on the mind and on the sub-conscious. However, if that is where they stay, the effect is quite limited. Affirmations, to truly work, must originate in your mind, but resonate in your gut…in your soul…in your Being.

I have tried affirming many things during my years of searching. However, only a few of them have taken root. When I started working with affirmations, I would say some things over and over again with no obvious change. That is because they only existed on the surface and as soon as I slipped back onto automatic pilot, the old messages would once again kick into gear.

Discouraged, I concluded that all my affirming and positive thinking had been pointless.

However, there have been some affirmations that I can feel all the way down to my toes every time I say them. I can feel them in my head. I can feel them in my heart. They are a part of me and the effects have been phenomenal. Let me give you some examples.

Many years ago we were in debt—big-time debt—and I worried about money ALL of the time. The fears kept me awake at night and never left me during the day. Eventually, I became desperate and felt like I would explode if I did not do something very soon. I came across an affirmation that I really desired to be true. I connected with it immediately and so when I was on my walks, or driving in the car, or doing house work, I would say it over and over again. Before long, I was saying it with feeling—slower and with more expression—and I began to feel it deep down inside of me instead of merely in my head, which is where it started. This was the affirmation:

The Universe is abundant.

Therefore, I am abundant.

All my wants and needs are amply met.

Within a surprisingly short period of time, I noticed that I was no longer worrying about money every day. John had decided to retire the following year, and without bringing home any additional money, he was paying off credit cards surprisingly fast. He amazed me. I saw my affirmation in action and saw what happens when one stops worrying and starts believing. The abundance came to us, when I KNEW that it would, and the Universe knew that I knew because my affirmation was now coming from deep within me.

I experienced the same result when I legally dropped my first name, Judith, and started using my former middle name, Marilyn, in 1996. To get used to my new name, I said "I am Marilyn" over and over and over again. With each repetition, I changed the emphasis on the various words. One day as I was saying my affirmation, I noticed that tears were running down my face, because I had become Marilyn in the deepest and most sensitive part of me. Now, when I say "I am Marilyn" I feel a reverence inside of me because it has permeated every pore of my body and every molecule of my Being.

I do not need to use these particular affirmations every day now because they have become a natural part of me. When I feel the need for confirmation, I say them a few times and realize that I still feel them deeply within me. When I try a new affirmation and it does not "feel" right almost immediately, I know that I am wasting my time because it will never be a part of me the way the ones mentioned above are.

Life is too short and we are too busy to waste our time affirming things that only resonate in our heads. If, after a while, you feel nothing, change the wording to make it more heartfelt, or let it go because, for some reason, you are not ready to alter that part of you just yet. Learn to know yourself and trust your intuition on such things. You are the most valuable tool you have, so make good use of all that is at your disposal. Only you know exactly what you need. Make your first affirmation one that affirms that knowledge and then just go where it leads you.

My List Of Affirmations

1.

2.

3.

4.

5.

6.

7.

8.

9.

10.

"BE ABSOLUTELY SURE YOU ARE WRONG, BEFORE YOU CHANGE YOUR MIND!"

This has nothing to do with being *right* as opposed to being *wrong*. This has to do with having faith in your own convictions while being true to yourself. As a people-pleaser (a most unbecoming characteristic in its extreme) I was very talented at predicting the moods, desires, and needs of everyone around me. This was a talent that I took to perfection, but in the end it wore me down and I knew that I had to make some changes.

I believe that one friend came into my life just to teach me this lesson. She was a person that I admired very much. People who saw us together said that I appeared to be absolutely awed by her. I remember sitting and talking to her for long hours at a stretch and loving every minute—as long as I was saying things that pleased her. When I said something that displeased her, she would wrinkle an eyebrow and say nothing, but I knew from that one gesture that I had better start back-pedaling and fast. I was so talented in my people-pleasing tricks that I could change my words in the middle of a sentence if I saw that brow beginning to furrow. Without saying anything, I changed my mind, even though I had been speaking my truth before the brow went into action. After the fact, I decided that this woman supposedly loved me because I had given her complete control over me.

As proof of this theory, our friendship ended when I told her my truth by letter while she was away for an extended holiday. Without the influence of her eyebrow showing me her disapproval, I gently and lovingly said something that I had to say. However, she did not want that from me. Our friendship was not based on truth between two people; it was based on her ability to make me change my mind to her way of thinking, even though I was not convinced that I had been wrong in the first place. I was like a puppet to her, and to please her, I danced for all I was worth.

This has been a very long and arduous lifetime lesson for me, and this friend was just one of many who have had this effect on me. Even though I am in total awareness of it now, I still have to make a conscious effort not to fall into the trap of selling myself short again. I thought that to agree with people at all times was to be loved by them. In that twisted way of thinking, I wonder how I ever thought that they would get to know me. It is also no wonder that I had trouble identifying who I was because I spent all my time thinking like others, changing my mind for others, and giving everyone else more power than I ever gave myself .

Questions To Consider

1. How has 'people-pleasing' affected your life? How would your life be different if you pleased yourself first?

2. Is there a difference between being a good and kind person and being a person who lives to please others? How do you know that you are being one or the other when it is happening?

3. Do you say what you want to say, or what others want to hear? Give your thoughts on this.

BELIEFS VS KNOWINGS

BELIEFS

Beliefs come to us through other people (parents, older siblings, teachers, clergy, spouses, friends, authority figures) and the younger we are when we receive them, the greater chance there is that they will stick with us for a very long time. A child can be led to believe anything about him or herself, especially if the point is repeated over and over again by an influential adult.

However, a *really* powerful negative statement can be just as permanent even though it is only uttered one time. For instance, if a child is told by a person of importance that he or she is ugly or stupid or unworthy of love *just one time* that becomes a belief that will stick like glue forever if nothing is done to change it. Unfortunately, powerful positive declarations are not usually turned into beliefs unless they are repeated to the child many, many times with no interruption from a negative statement. Until we become very aware of this phenomenon and take control of it in our own lives, the tendency is to believe negative statements about ourselves more readily than we believe the positive ones.

Sometimes the message comes through in an action rather than in words. For instance, if a child is left alone day after day, the message he or she learns is "I am unlovable. No one wants to spend time with me." I was issued an unusual punishment as a two-year-old that affected the way I viewed life and other people for the next fifty years. The message I received from that action, which occurred just one time in my life, reached far and wide, and I still occasionally react to it to this day. In fact, my response to my mother's action that day became the basis for my entire belief system. Never underestimate the power of single deed! (*The story of this incident is explained in my book Free at Last My Journey Into, Through and Out of Depression.*)

Most beliefs limit us because we change the way we would normally do things in order to uphold what we have been taught; some of these are real gems that stop us in our tracks. Here is an example of something that was not even said maliciously; it was just a statement that I accepted without question. One day when I was a teenager, in reaction to something I was having trouble doing, my mother told me very quietly, "Judy, you have very little stamina." I must have wanted an excuse to not have to do anything physical because that kept me out of anything that required much energy for a very long time. I felt fragile and weak and in need of protection. It was not even an unkind statement; apparently, it was merely a fact that day.

What would have been different in my life if Mom had worded it this way, "Judy, why don't you take a break? You work so hard, but right now you need a rest." Wow! What could I have done in my life that I missed out on doing because I was sure that I did not have the energy to do it?

A few years ago, my husband told me that I was quitter, because I would start a project and then as soon as I became proficient at it, I would quit. He said that he did not think that there was anything I could not do, but when I tried to do it, I never finished. For the next few weeks, I stopped doing any hobbies because of his words. I believed him, so to speak. I let him make me believe that I was a quitter—for a while. One day I said to him, "John, how can I ever find what I am supposed to be doing if I don't give everything a try? I am searching and I will know my heart's work when I find it. When something special touches my heart I know I won't be able to quit. There must be a void in me that I keep trying to fill, but I'm not going to let your opinion about this stop me anymore." He smiled and said, "I had no idea that you were searching for anything. I thought you just wanted something to do. I won't call you a quitter ever again." He kept his word. What actually happened is that the *belief* I formed because of his words, turned into a knowing because of my own.

In conclusion, a belief comes from someone else and it is changeable. This applies to all beliefs, even the ones that seem to be carved in stone. Look back on your life and see the beliefs that have changed for you along the way.

KNOWINGS

A knowing is one of the most wonderful feelings in the world—especially a newly discovered one! A knowing is yours alone. It does not matter whether anyone else in the whole world shares it with you or not. You know it in the deepest part of you and that is what makes it so powerful. No one can talk you out of it and for some reason, when you have a knowing, people very rarely even try to challenge it. On some level, they too, know that you know!

People mirror to me what they see in me and often this is a subconscious exchange. I have been challenged about my beliefs, but that is probably because I was questioning them, too, and it showed. I have never been questioned on a knowing. I obviously have projected the message that the topic of my knowing is not up for discussion and so that is accepted by others on a subconscious level.

Knowings are felt deep down inside of me like a delicious secret that I have with God. Knowings make me feel strong and wise. A knowing is also an accomplishment because it only comes from life learnings (that are often painful) and there is a feeling of having earned it. Here are a few examples of **my** knowings:

- ✦ I know that every person on Earth is equal.
- ✦ I know that when a child is hurt on the other side of the world, I feel it in some way.
- ✦ I know that we are all part of a Master Plan.
- ✦ I know that I am a worthy, loving and lovable person.
- ✦ I know that I have a purpose in life that is unique because my combination of talents is like no other.
- ✦ I know that each person in my life was chosen by me for very good reasons.
- ✦ I know that I have gifts and talents that come through me rather than from me,
- ✦ I know that I am an international author and speaker.

These are some of the things that I know about life from where I am standing. Your vantage point is different than mine and so your knowings will be different; you are seeing the world from your own life experience.

Questions

1. What do you **believe** about yourself?

2. What do you **know** about yourself?

The subconscious believes what it hears, not necessarily what is true.

3. What has your subconscious believed because it was heard, not because it was true?

4. What beliefs about you could you choose to change, discard, or form into knowings?

BOUNDARIES AND COMFORT ZONES

We all have boundaries, but for the most part we are unaware of them. For many years, I knew what made me feel uncomfortable, but I did not understand what was happening at those times. Now that I am becoming more aware of the things that cause me discomfort, I have learned that I have a boundary that says *I do not like people sitting or standing too close to me.* I need some distance between us or I cannot even concentrate on what they are saying. I have boundaries that say that *no man other than my husband can touch my body* (except for a heartfelt hug). I have boundaries that say *that I will do much for you when it comes from MY heart, but do not Expect it from me.* And still another boundary is that I will not accept disrespectful language from you in reference to me. *I do not accept rudeness from anyone.*

I have boundaries that will *not let me intentionally break the law*—neither Universal nor societal. I have boundaries that will *not let me be less than honest in important matters.* I can cheat no one and will not allow the state of being a victim into my range of possibilities. I have moderate boundaries when it comes to outsiders being in my living space for lengthy periods of time. To accommodate this, I have arranged my home accordingly. I have slight boundaries on the showing of emotion. I have no boundaries on how much I can give to or how much I can love another human being or animal.

Boundaries protect us in good ways, but they can also be harmful if they are as immovable as a brick wall. The good boundaries are tools that indicate when someone has stepped over the line of appropriate conduct. All good relationships involve at least two people who have made known their expectations of the other (even unconsciously) and the limits of what they will knowingly tolerate. When they do not have this knowledge about one another, trouble begins. In a healthy relationship, one party can tell the other when that line has been crossed, and it becomes a lesson learned as opposed to an obstacle that cannot be overcome. A boundary is basically the limit of what you will accept from another person, or what you will give out yourself.

Boundaries are different from comfort zones. A *boundary* has to do with our morals and acceptance (or not) of what other people give/do to us. A *comfort zone* has to do with our degree of willingness to participate as individuals in the world. Comfort zones are like elastic bands. The more we stretch in our actions, the bigger our comfort zones become.

For instance—let us picture a housewife/mother who has spent years talking only to her children, husband, and other family members. Then one day she joins the Parent & Teacher Association (PTA) and speaks up about something she believes in. She is sure that no one wants to hear her opinion, but she gives it anyway. That stretches her comfort zone. Then she becomes President of the PTA and has to speak at the meetings every week. Her comfort zone is now much bigger. Before long someone persuades her to run for city council. This is a big stretch and she is afraid; she does it and is elected. Her comfort zone is now larger than she ever dreamed possible. She is dealing with crowds of people and officials of government every day. She is handling problems that she could never even have imagined when she was a stay-at-home mom. The more she handles, the more she *can* handle, and that is because her zone of comfort has increased many-fold.

Boundaries and Comfort Zones

1. Make a list of boundaries that you know you have.

2. Which of your boundaries listed in #1 support your growth and which ones hinder it?

3. What have you done lately that has increased the diameter of your comfort zone?

4. Have you turned down any life-altering opportunities out of fear of stretching beyond your zone of comfort?

5. What could you do that would change one of your hindering *boundaries*? What would you be *willing* to do?

FAITH

My faith has often felt like an ebb tide—going in and going out depending on what is happening in my life. When the events of my life overwhelm me, my tide of faith, rolls out to sea, leaving only a lonely sandy shore in its wake. If I chance to look for my faith, all that I might see are the broken bits and pieces that become lodged in the sand before the main tide breaks away. As things slow down and as I become more mentally aware of my spiritual Being once more, I feel the wave of faith pound back onto the shores of my soul. There it stays until the next crisis occurs.

This is a very poor picture of faith—*doubting* in the bad times, and *believing* when things feel good. In other word, it is having "a fair weather friendship with God." Since realizing that, I have worked very hard to turn the ebb tide into a peaceful river that flows constantly through me, always changing, but never disappearing as the tides had formerly done. There have been days when the level of the river is dangerously low, but I have never experienced a drought, not even in the most troubling days.

Faith is one of the most misunderstood aspects of the human experience. We have all heard the term, "doubting Thomas." For those who are familiar with the Bible, the story of this man's lack of faith is well documented. For others, suffice it to say that faith depends on the willingness to acknowledge that there are powers in this Universe far beyond the capabilities of any human being. If there is any doubt about that, just look out your window and see the flower that comes back year after year; or the robin that finds its way back to your yard every spring, after being away all winter.

Faith that needs proof is not faith at all. I love the saying, "Faith begins where knowledge ends." Faith does not have to involve God as such, but it does have to involve "something bigger than you or I." Faith is that wonderful knowledge that no matter what happens I am never alone. I will never be left without my inner resources and I will never have to handle anything bigger than my capabilities will allow. Faith lets me feel peace in the midst of a storm. Faith is that assurance that I am loved (in the deepest part of me) no matter how chaotic my world or the world around me becomes. This marvel can be summed up in the following phrase:

> **"If you knew who walks beside you,
> you would never be afraid again."**

(Adapted from a quote by Wayne Dyer)

As you can choose to have joy in your life, so can you choose to have faith in your heart. Once you choose it, however, you will be tested over and over again, until one day faith has become a natural part of you. The reason I know this to be true is that it has been my experience that the people who have known the most hardships in life are often the ones who have the most faith. I, myself, am still being tested to see if my faith is truly a river now, or whether it still has the tendency to become that ebb tide that flows in and out with the struggles of my life. I feel that it has finally become a river, but I still welcome the tests, because I feel exhilarated whenever I am made to acknowledge the faith within me once more. Faith in all that is good gives me the comfort of returning home after a hard day out in the world.

Faith

1. Is your faith like a tide or like a river? If neither, what does it look like?

2. Tell about a time when your faith was put to the test and your faith shone through.

3. Tell about a time when you found yourself face-to-face with a struggle and felt starved of faith.

4. Put into words (for your eyes only) what faith means to you. What do you have faith in? How does faith fit into your everyday life? How can you put more faith into your life?

FEAR ELIMINATES FAITH.
FAITH ELIMINATES FEAR.

FEAR

AAAAAAH—the topic on which I am an expert! I have lived with fear for so long that I used to think that I invented it. Night and day, I had unnamed, unnecessary, and non-sensible stress inside of me. After a while it became normal and I took little notice of it. A day seemingly *free of fear* became just another *source of fear* for me. Then, on March 29, 1984, I finally collapsed completely and was in and out of hospitals for the next three years. I was prescribed multiple pills, but still the fear persisted. I alienated many people I knew, and after years of living in my own version of Hell, I decided to do something about it. The pills were not helping, so what would help?

Slowly I started looking into my fear (for me, it has been in the form of *terror*) and realized that fear has many faces. It can look like anger, frustration, doubt, procrastination, promiscuity, obsessions, addictions, and all manner of other negative characteristics. People use these methods to stop feeling afraid, but none of them work—some delay the inevitable, but none are cures since they are all forms of fear themselves.

One of the best days of my life was when I realized that *looking at it, talking to it*, and then *going through it* was the one and only sure way to conquer a fear. As soon as I looked a fear in the eye, it became smaller; when I talked to it, it diminished some more, and by the time I went through it, it had all but disappeared. Of course, the hardest part in the process is to make the decision to take that first look. After that, the process takes on a life of its own and becomes easier. One thing that increased my desire to deal with my fears was the statement "Fear and guilt cannot co-exist with love." That really upset me because I considered myself to be a loving person but that was good, because it motivated me to do some effective soul-searching.

Fear can be a paralyzer. I have let more dreams slip through my fingers due to paralyzing fear than for any other reason. When I stopped to figure out what I was really afraid of, it was usually something very small or else totally indefinable because it was irrational. However, since most of our basic fears are born in us during childhood, we must remember that to a child everything is big, and everything is scary. The fears belong to the child within, and so they feel more intense and much larger than they would be to an adult.

I have learned a lot about fear from my two dogs. Our female, Ceili, used to be afraid of anything that was unfamiliar. The dogs had decided what their world looked like and when something new showed up, Ceili, more than her brother, Newton, went berserk. One day we parked a bike by the fence and, when she noticed it, she cried as though her world had gone to pieces. I took her over to the bike, let her sniff it, touch it, and then she was never bothered by it again, Once she was acquainted with it, she could accept it. Around that same time, if she saw a piece of paper flitting about where none had flitted before, she became afraid. Once again, when I put her into direct contact with it, she was fine. With my help, Ceili was able to look squarely at the source of her fears, and because a dog's brain is not as cluttered as a human one, she was able to deal with it very quickly.

In truth, we humans handle many of our fears the same way. Once we understand something, it is not as scary as before. However, there is another kind of fear that Ceili illustrated for me as well. She had a fear that made no sense and no matter what I did she could not seem to get past it. She was afraid of the toilet paper on the roll-holder in the bathroom. I let her smell it, touch it, even pull on it—but when left alone, she still went crazy barking at it in her most fearful voice. There was no explanation for the prolonged fear, and thus, it resembled the kind that does the most damage in humans. These are the terrors that need to be looked at, but usually are not, and it is in these supposedly unexplained fears, that dwells the greatest chance for victory.

Fears are worth talking about in depth because they encompass so much. They are the basis of our negative self-talk; they are the reasons we indulge in sabotage; they are the reasons our ego gets to win over our spirit so very often. Fears are powerful and can do irreparable damage if allowed to persist.

PLEASE NOTE:

I am not concerned at this time with the fears that invoke taking unnecessary risks. For instance, I am afraid of bungee jumping, but I have decided that this is a fear that I will just have to live with. I am not talking about the fears that are good fears—those that keep us from walking out into the path of a speeding vehicle. I am talking about the fears that stop us from succeeding at life—the unfounded fears that began probably before we even have memory.

REMEMBER:

Fear can take many forms:

Terror	Anxiety and stress	Phobias	Anger
Jealousy	Extreme Doubt	Inability to Commit	Sabotage
Depression	Shame	Guilt	Distrust

1. What forms of fear do you have in your life? What is the most obvious one?

2. Close your eyes and try to visualize the fear within you. Write about what you see and describe it as clearly as possible.

3. What has fear stopped you from doing in your daily life?

4. What are the pay offs that come from having this fear?

5. How would your life be different if you had no terror, no anger, no jealousy, no need to control, and no guilt?

6. Are you willing to look one of your fears in the eye as a first step in letting it go? If so, which fear are you ready to let go of?

7. List the things you are afraid to do out in the world.

Describe the terrors that affect you in the following areas:
    Physical
    Emotional/Mental
    Spiritual.

FORGIVENESS

To forgive another person is to free yourself! *To be forgiven* is a gift of inner joy! We humans with our highly developed brains have the ability to hurt one another out of thoughtlessness as well as with malicious intent. No other species on Earth does that to its own kind for those reasons. Other animals may destroy one another, but that is part of their nature, and not something involving feelings or intent. We say that we love one another unconditionally, but our actions prove otherwise. If we really did practice unconditional love, forgiveness would be unnecessary.

What is forgiveness? To forgive another person is to open one's heart and give love to someone that we have formerly allowed to hurt us. No one can hurt us without our permission, so in essence we are also forgiving ourselves for letting it happen. The person who has been forgiven then has to choose to let the guilt go. How many times have you heard someone say, "I have been forgiven for what I did, but I just can't forgive myself"? I am sure that most of us have said that at one time or another. It is not easy to let yourself off the proverbial hook if you have done something to hurt someone else, but why would you want to stay there—especially if the other person has given you permission to get on with your life without the burden of the guilt anymore.

Much energy is spent on past deeds that one has done in error or, worse, with intent. If true remorse is there, then growth can occur, and anything that brings about growth cannot be bad. However, if a person who has committed a wrong continues to justify why he did it or claims that he had no choice in the matter, there most likely will be no forgiveness, no growth, and a spiritual opportunity will have been missed.

Apologizing is something that we humans do not do well. If an apology contains the word "but," then it is not an apology, it is an explanation. A true apology says, "I am sorry for_____." **No explanation.** It could be simply, "I am sorry for hurting you. I ask for your forgiveness." ***Do Not use the word "but" in an apology***.

The word "but" negates all that has gone before. If you say, "I am sorry for hurting you, **but** (I was under a lot of pressure that day)." the sincerity is lost. Once a qualification or explanation is added it means that you are justifying what you said or did. You may add another sentence as long as "but" is not present or implied. "I am sorry for being so mean to you. You did not deserve it."

Forgiveness

1. Tell about something in your life that you are hanging onto even though you said that you forgave the person who did it to you.

2. Write about something that you have apologized for and for which you have been granted forgiveness, but that you cannot forgive yourself for doing.

3. Is there something you should be apologizing for, but have not? Why not?

4. Has anyone asked for your forgiveness, but you refused to give it? Why?

5. Has anyone refused to forgive you after you have asked for it? Why do you think he or she would refuse?

GRATITUDE

Gratitude is one of the reasons that the planet keeps rotating on its axes. A really bad day can be made better by someone giving you a heartfelt "thank you." You can change someone's whole outlook by praising them and expressing your appreciation to them. Gratitude makes even the one who is grateful feel better about life. Imagine a world where every person thanked God or the Universe every day for even one thing. There would be no more wars, no more violence, and no more dysfunctional families. Yes, gratitude is *that* powerful.

I am grateful for my life and everything in it—good, bad, and everything in between. Whenever I am feeling down, I feel better as soon as I utter a few quiet words of thanksgiving for something—anything. Thankfulness is its own "pick-me-up." Lately, when I find myself doubting my ability to successfully complete some aspect of my work, I say a quiet thank you for the talents and gifts that I have; that silences the negative voice inside me for a while.

Gratitude is the energy that makes it possible for me to get up each morning. I am grateful to my Creator for giving me life and good health and an insatiable appetite for my own truth. I am grateful to the people in my life who daily cross my path and who give me lessons, some easy and some more difficult, but all welcomed and all valued. Ultimately, I am grateful to the people around me who let me know that I have made a difference in their lives. Being needed and appreciated is an essential part of living.

I gave my very first talk at a halfway house in Edmonton. After the session, a scruffy man (who liked to be called "Gramps") met me at the door on my way out and handed me a little card that read:

"To Marilyn,

You are so special.

Thank you for the wonderful gift you have given me.

Gramps"

I did not read it until I got to my car and when I ran back to thank him, he was gone. I sent him a card to tell him how much his words meant to me and told him how he had touched my soul with his innocent and heartfelt gratitude. Apparently my words of sincere appreciation made him feel important; made him feel visible; made him feel special. I was told that he was inspired to make a few positive changes in his life, and although I am writing about it, I take no credit for that because he gave me an even bigger gift. He confirmed for me that I was on the right path and that my work would make a difference. He also reminded me that a few words of gratitude can change lives. You never know when that will be the case, so never miss a chance when the opportunity lies before you. Sometimes we think something is too small to say "thank you" for, but that is never the case. Everyone needs to experience that special feeling that only comes when someone says "thank you" and means it. And best of all, you will never know from where the gratitude will come. Of all the men in that room whom I thought would have been grateful, Gramps would have been the last. He did not smile at me or make eye contact even once the whole time I was there.

SUGGESTION

As recommended by Sarah Ban Braethnach in her books about gratitude, before you go to sleep each night, say thank you for at least 5 lessons that you have received during that day. No matter whether you write them or just say them; God likes to be appreciated.

HONESTY

I have been accused of being honest in almost every circle or group to which I have belonged—I have to assume that that is a compliment, but on one or two occasions it has not felt that way. Sometimes people do not want to hear what someone else has to say about them. After having a few putdowns for just blurting out what I thought, I now try to wait until the other person asks me for my thoughts about his or her problems. It works much better that way. I *am* honest, most of the time. The honesty that I have trouble with is the surface kind. For instance, if a friend's hair looks terrible, what is the point of telling her so—especially if the problem cannot be easily fixed! If *asked* for a truthful opinion, I would find a kind way of saying that her hair has seen better days.

I am much more able to be honest about important things—I could not tell my husband a lie, if it was to save my own life. I cannot keep anything from him, so I am not even capable of lying by omission. If someone is talking to me about his or her problems and he or she truly wants my help, I am very honest because to be anything else would defeat the purpose of talking to me. I am honest in financial transactions and if a salesperson gives me too much change or charges me less than the going price, I always rectify the situation. More than likely the error will come out of the person's wages if nothing is said. However, this does not earn bragging rights since one should not be congratulated for doing something that is just the right thing to do. Honesty should be so commonplace that a person would not think to write about it. Unfortunately, that is not the case in this world.

Honesty

1. In your heart of hearts, do you consider yourself to be an honest person? If not, why not?

2. Put down your thoughts about what honesty means to you.

3. Have you ever been around a dishonest person for any length of time? Explain.

4. Tell about a time when you were dishonest with someone.

5. Tell about a situation in which you have been dishonest with yourself.

6. Where is the line that you draw between honesty and dishonesty?

7. Is "surface truth" worth it even if it hurts someone's feelings? Explain.

8. Is it acceptable to be dishonest as long as no one else finds out about it? Why or why not?

JEALOUSY

Jealousy is pain in action. It is one of the two man-made emotions (the other being GUILT) and it is as ugly to observe, as it is to experience. A person who feels extremely jealous feels unworthy of love or attention and cannot abide seeing anyone else receiving them either. If the pain of this form of fear could be measured on the Richter scale, it would register as being an earthquake of major proportions. Jealousy shows no reason and can be very dangerous in the extreme.

Envy is a mild form of jealousy and probably everyone has felt it at some time or other. When my husband used to be away working ALL of the time, I envied those women whose spouses were home every night. Sometimes, they confided in me that they were envious of me because I had time for myself. I have been envious of people who appeared to have no financial difficulties when I felt like we had so many. When we lived in a rented condominium, I envied people who owned their own homes. The envy did me no good, but it did no one else any harm either.

Jealousy is another matter because it hurts both the bearer of the jealousy and the person who is the target of the negativity. I have been jealous when I have seen my husband dance more than one dance with another woman. I have been jealous when someone I knew accomplished something that I desperately wanted to do. All that negativity made me feel as though I was going to explode inside.

Jealousy is an outward sign of inadequacy and self-loathing. I would not be jealous if I felt secure in my abilities to keep my husband interested in me. Was my self-estimation so low that I thought two dances with someone else would erase his love for me and all of our years together? Apparently so, because as I stood watching them I remember fear going through me like a burning knife. When a friend accomplished the thing that I had wanted to do, I got angry because I felt useless and I was sure that if I ever did accomplish the feat, no one would think it was a big deal at all because she had done it first. I wanted to do something unique because I desperately needed to be seen, to be noticed. I often felt invisible and this action of hers brought that inadequacy to the forefront. As I said, jealousy is the not the voice of reason.

Thankfully, I do not experience jealousy to that extent anymore. I admit to having momentary lapses, but nothing that cannot be dealt with as soon as I feel those familiar twinges begin to creep over me. Now I trust the process of my life. I have learned my own value and know that I am on my own path. I no longer depend on others to take care of my every need. I also know that my gifts may appear to be like someone else's, but they are not the same. The fact that no one else has seen the world from my perspective gives me unique talents to offer the world; likewise, my friend, and every other person. When I learned to love myself, I stopped being jealous of everyone else around me.

Jealousy is useless. If I do find myself feeling any of those dreaded insecurities, I ask myself why I have brought this situation into my life. What lessons am I supposed to learn from it? As soon as I take responsibility for what happens to me, the power of the fear dissipates. The jealousy becomes non-existent. I know that only I can activate the jealousy in me, and only I can send it away.

Jealousy

1. What have you been envious or jealous of in your life?

2. Do you have a jealous person in your life? If yes, what is that like?

3. Write all you can about your jealousy. Use another sheet of paper if necessary.

4. What are the payoffs for this emotion?

5. How could you lessen the feelings of jealousy that you experience?

OUR PLACE IN THE WORLD

Every action we do affects every other person on Earth. We can feel the pain (although I do not believe it comes across as the *same* pain) of a child who is hurting or starving on the other side of the world. Our attitudes travel like ripples in all directions and affect millions. So with that in mind, our first step toward being of service to the world is to clean up our own personal thoughts, feelings, and attitudes.

How can we expect peace in the world if we do not even live in peace with our neighbors, our friends, and our family?

How can we worry about why there are starving children in the world if we have not even wondered why we have starving children in our own community?

How can we worry about Canada or the USA going to war with Iraq or any other country when some of us are in constant struggle with our neighbors or families?

How can we worry about being kind to the homeless person on the street when we are sometimes unkind to the person we supposedly love the most in the world?

As long as we think in terms of "they" and "we" on any issue, we will never know peace. Peace begins in one heart at a time and it takes on a ripple effect from there.

Questions

1. Look at your home life—is there peace in your home? Is it truly your haven? What do you do to "keep the peace"? What could you change that would improve the peaceful quality of your home-life?

2. List the ways you could actively create peace in your own neighborhood.

3. Would you consider yourself to be a peacemaker? Why or why not?

4. How far would you have to go to step out of your comfort zone with regard to the above questions?

Hint: List things that you know could be done to promote peace in your world, but which you are nervous or afraid to do.

PASSIONS

To do something with passion is to do it with love. All of my passions originate in my soul and are as natural as the blood that is pumped through my heart every minute of every day. When I am paying attention to what makes me happy, I am open to knowing my passions.

For all of my early life I knew that I was here on this Earth for a very good and very specific reason. The years went steadily by and after surviving mental illness, I was more convinced than ever that there was *something* I was supposed to be doing (but I had no idea what it could be). I tried every kind of hobby that I could think of and while I excelled at some of them, the interest always wore off, even though I spent loads of money trying to make them happen. My starting and stopping of hobbies, including buying all of the best equipment, was so well-known that someone once said to me, "If you ever decide to try painting, let me know when it wears off—I would love to have all those supplies you'll be buying." Talk about being predictable!

When I was talking about *Beliefs and Knowings*, I told you how my husband labeled me a quitter and told me that I must be afraid of succeeding because I never took any project to completion. I did not want to be thought of in that way, especially by him, so I stopped doing anything that was creative because I knew I would not want to do it forever. However, about a year ago, I came to a life-changing conclusion—I am not a quitter; I am a relentless searcher. In the past, I did always lose interest, but that was my clue that these crafts were not passions; they were things to do until something better came along. The more ventures I eliminated, the closer I was getting to what I was supposed to be doing.

In 2002, out of the blue, I began public speaking. I then put together my book of poetry which is called <u>The Girl Behind the Closed Door</u>. I was crazy into writing at that time and ultimately, I began to put this book together for workshops. I get tired **from** doing these things, but I never grow tired **of** doing them. I know these are my passions because they make my heart purr. Now, my only problem is to try to balance my passions with other important things like home, family and friends.

Now I know that my passions have been with me from day one. I have always loved being the center of attention and absolutely love talking to groups of people. I have always been a writer and a poet. I have always been a searcher of truth and that is what I talk about. These things come easily to me. I may learn to do them better over time and with more experience, but I do not need to go out and take any courses to do them. They are a part of me, like breathing and being!

People form businesses based on what they love to do or what they would like to see improved in the world. If a person takes the liberty of choosing a career or a vocation, they choose something that they at least like to do. Those who are very fortunate know what they *love* to do and so make a career of that. I did not realize until recently that the things that are the easiest and that have been there all along are the things that compose our passions. I thought life had to be harder than that! My spiritual obligation is to love my life and to use all the gifts that have been so graciously and generously given to me. I am grateful for that all that I am.

Questions

1. Name at least five things that you have done easily all of your life.

    1)

    2)

    3)

    4)

    5)

2. Are you doing work that makes you happy and excited? If not, why not?

3. Are you using any of the five things in #1 in your work? If not, why not?

4. Write yourself a letter yourself about your passions. Use a full sheet of paper for this. Put it in an envelope and mail it to yourself.

PATTERNS

Patterns are guides that help us to do an action over and over again in exactly the same way that we did it the very first time. By choosing to follow a pattern, we are saying that its action works for us and achieves what we have set out to accomplish. This is wonderful when we are sewing clothes or following a recipe, but what about those patterns in life that we habitually follow and then miserably complain about. A pattern can only be changed when we acknowledge and take responsibility for its existence.

"Insanity is doing the same action over and over again and each time expecting a different result." Einstein coined these timeless and wise words that we can all learn. We all have these patterns in our lives and one interesting facet of them is that they are only repeatable if you are not aware that you are using them. For example:

"A man comes home from work at exactly 5 PM every day. Like clockwork, he walks in and announces that he is home and he wants his supper immediately. His wife comes out and says that supper will be ready soon. He yells that he has been working hard all day and deserves his supper when he walks in the door. They argue heatedly, eventually eat their meal in stony silence, and then spend the evening bickering. They go to bed, still angry, and the next day it starts all over again."

"A sleepy old dog lies out in front of his owner's shop all day every day. Also, with daily frequency, an old man goes to that shop to buy his newspaper. Without fail, as he gets to the shop, he does not see the dog and so he trips over him, kicking him soundly as he does so. Every day the dog jumps up and bites him. As though it had never happened before, the old man walks home with his paper under his arm, all the while cursing the mangy mutt who attacked him."

"Every evening a man sits and reads the daily newspaper before dinner. As soon as he sits down, his wife joins him and begins to tell him all about her day. He grunts occasionally just so that she thinks he is listening. She soon realizes that he is not hearing her, and so she stomps away feeling mad and hurt and totally unloved. They spend the evening—

every evening—in silence."

These are fictional, but possible, examples that could be a fact in any of our lives. A pattern can be rendered inoperable at any time by merely *changing one detail, one time.* That is all it takes to shut it down forever. In the first example, the wife could go to her husband when he comes in the door and say, "Hi, Honey, you're looking really tired. Why don't you go clean up and I'll have your dinner ready as soon as you're done." Or what would change if, when he came in, he said, "Hi, Dear, how was your day? Do I have time to get cleaned up before we eat?" It would then be impossible for the rest of the evening to play out as it always had before because at least one of the cues has been changed. However, if they really want to be miserable to one another, they will have subconsciously created a back-up plan that will automatically come out in the event that they eliminate the original one. The reason why a pattern is allowed to continue is that it serves a purpose. Sometimes, people do not know how to be anything but unhappy, and so they set up a pattern of action that will keep them feeling miserable but comfortable. (If asked, they would probably state that they were happy!)

Questions

1. How could the patterns be broken in the second and third examples?

2. What patterns do you want to change in your life and why do you think you created them?

3. Figure out one pattern in your life and re-write the script. Remember, if it involves even one other person, you are only free to change YOUR OWN lines.

PEACE

Peace is what LIFE is all about. Even when we are not aware of it, I think that we are all searching for that elusive butterfly … inner peace. How do I search for something that I am not sure I would recognize even if it landed on my shoulder and whispered, "I am Peace"? Every major religion in the world incorporates the concept of peace into its core. Even atheists yearn for this glorious state of being that originates from deep within and radiates outwards. When asked, some people may perhaps say that good health is their most ardent wish, but after some consideration, they might possibly change their minds. Without a doubt, good health is of utmost importance, but if you have true peace, then you will be able to handle anything that comes your way, including ill health. In my opinion, peace overrides everything and cannot be improved upon or replaced by anything else.

Peace is a state of being that … just is. There are no words to adequately describe it, but it is similar to *love* in that even if you do not know what to expect beforehand, when you have it, you know it! I used to think that peace was something that could only be achieved when and if I solved all the problems of my world and then moved onto a mountaintop. Even then, I would think peace would only be possible if I learned how to meditate. I have always had trouble meditating, so I had resigned myself to never knowing peace.

Have you ever gone through a time when you have been wrestling within yourself about some important issue and the more you struggle, the more out of control you feel? Perhaps you are trying to decide on something that will change your life and the lives of those around you. You feel overwhelmed by the magnitude of what lies before you and all of a sudden, you know that you cannot win, at least not by yourself. The moment you accept your powerlessness and hand the problem over to a Greater Power, you experience a feeling of bliss, which is the first dawning of peace.

After a weekend at a workshop where I became intimately aware of my soul (or my Being), I edged very close to truly understanding this concept of peace. I still did not think that it was mine for the taking because I was still not able to sit quietly for more than a few minutes. However, I felt better just knowing more about myself on such a deep level. One day shortly after the seminar, I had a most profound, memorable, yet simple experience. As I was taking the clothes out of the washer and putting them into the dryer, I had nothing on my mind except the task at hand. I was immersed in lifting the clothes out of the washer and putting them into the dryer. Lift out—put in—lift out—put in. That is all that I was doing. Quietly, with no fanfare, I heard the words in my mind, "So this is what Peace feels like!" In that split moment, I figured it out. Peace occurs whenever you are TOTALLY—not mostly—in the present. At that moment, there is no past and no future. There are no other places to be or tasks to do. *Being present in the moment* with every fiber of my being is PEACE. Wow!

Self-reflecting on Peace

1. What does PEACE mean to you?

2. Have you ever known PEACE in the true sense of the word?

3. Is there any difference between being at PEACE and feeling peaceful?

4. What could you do to promote PEACE in your life?

Place of picture of yourself as a child (preferably under 10 years of age) on this page. Spend some time looking at this image.

1. What passions did this child have?

2. Would he/she be happy with what you have done with your life?

3. What dreams did he/she have that you have fulfilled? Have not fulfilled?

4. As you study this picture, what is this child saying to you?

5. What characteristics did this child have that you have not?

DO NOT LOOK AT THE NEXT PAGE UNTIL THESE
QUESTIONS HAVE BEEN ANSWERED.
ON YOUR HONOR, PLEASE.

Using the hand you **DO NOT** normally write with, write a letter *to yourself from the child* on the previous page.

PRETEND YOU KNOW

You know more than you think you do! As children, we have all played "pretend." In that wonderful game, it is amazing to see the accuracy of the roles that we play just for fun. Then we become adults and something serious happens to us. We think that everyone else knows more than we do and we think that if we have not learned it from a source outside of ourselves, then it cannot be true.

During a seminar in 1999, the facilitator asked me a question and I replied, "I don't know!" She then said to me three powerful little words, *"Pretend you know."* Without missing a beat, I came up with an answer that made perfect sense and actually turned out to be right *for me*. Since then, I have used this method in my counseling and in my everyday life. To me, it is magic!

I was afraid of not knowing the correct answer, but by pretending, I peeled away the seriousness and discovered an answer that had been inside me all along. I did not even do much thinking; the answer was right there for the taking! What this tells me is that we are all afraid of being wrong and worse yet, having others find out about it. Also, we are much too serious about life and death and all the details in between. Children pretend so easily. I am sad to realize that in every child's life there must be a day when he or she is told that life is not a game of pretend, and so it is mandatory to stop playing it. I wonder if that is also the day when we learn that there is only one right way to do anything and to be wrong is a very bad thing—to be wrong in front of the world is intolerable. What a day that must have been each of us! No wonder we have chosen to forget it!

I have also used this method in completing the writing and compiling of my books and the composing and learning of my speeches. I had the desire and the inclination to do these things, but not all the knowledge I needed on how to do them. Therefore, on many occasions I have stumbled on an unknown and I have decided to just pretend that I know how to overcome it. Strangely enough, it was apparent that I knew more than I thought I did about each area of concern. By pretending to know, I found out that I did know!

Pretend You Know

In the coming weeks, I urge you to use this trick every chance you get. It will actually open up facets of your world that you did not even realize existed for you. When you let yourself pretend that you know, I would suggest that you make it feel like a lark—like a game—rather than trying too hard. Let yourself slip into the mindset that you had as a child when you made believe that you were someone different than who you were, doing things you supposedly knew nothing about. You did it then, you can do it now! You do know it all on some level. Why not let that part of you come out after being cooped up and ignored inside of you for so long? We all have the ability to do this, so lets do it!

PROCRASTINATION

Two months ago, I put a note on the wall to remind myself to write a piece on *"procrastination"* for this workbook. Well, today I am finally getting around to it! I wonder why it took me so long to address it. You probably would not believe me if I said that I *never* delay doing anything, and I did it just this once so I would have something to write about.

PRO-CRAS-TIN-ATION—it even sounds like a word that should be left until later. It sounds heavy and almost sinful. It makes me want to break a rule. It sounds like it should be rebelled against. Just looking at it and describing it, makes me want to put off discussing what it really means to me!

I have procrastinated when I was feeling mad at the whole world. I have procrastinated when everything around me made me feel really happy. I have procrastinated when I was alone and feeling detached from everyone. I have procrastinated when I was surrounded by throngs of people and feeling things were just too boring or too cumbersome to bother completing! (Yawn!) I have this huge urge to just stop typing right now, but I guess I have to finish this because if I stop, it will be waiting for me tomorrow.

Yes, I am having a little fun with the fact that we all procrastinate once in a while, but in actuality, it is not a fun trait, nor is it an inconsequential one. Habitual procrastinators are very difficult to live with and almost impossible to work with because they have no concept of deadlines or goals. I admit that we all do this dastardly deed from time to time, and as long as only small things are put off, there is probably not too much harm done. However, there is more to procrastination that meets the eye for those who do it on a regular basis.

Procrastination is a fear-based emotion that serves to postpone the inevitable because the person is afraid of seeing what the inevitable might be. It could be a part of the "I am a failure, so why not prove it?" frame of mind. There could also be an element of putting off even attempting a project so that you never have to let the world know that you do not know how to do it; or perhaps, even worse, that you do

People will delay looking for new jobs even though they complain bitterly about their present ones. Basically, they are terrified that they (or another person) will discover that they are not qualified for anything else. They are comfortable in the drudgery of all that bothers them in the old setting because they know what to expect there. The unfamiliarity and uncertainty of a change are just too scary to deal with, and so they put off the search. Many people are stuck in very deep ruts in jobs that they hate just because they are afraid of taking the risk of looking for a new one.

Any time that I have procrastinated doing something, I have found that the delayed activity grows in my mind until I get it done. I compare it to the ugly scary things that grow right in front of our eyes in a horror movie. The incomplete activity just gets bigger and bigger and BIGGER! Once I attack it—and that is what it feels like if I put it off long enough—I am always amazed at how easy it is and how little time it actually took. I always wonder afterwards why I did not do it sooner. Whatever I have been afraid of disappears immediately as soon as I resolve to do the dreaded task. Even writing this page turned out to be not so difficult at all.

A note to remember: There are many things that do not have to get done right away and you will know what things they are by how you feel about delaying them. They usually do not even come to mind again, until one day when you decide to do them. You will know you are procrastinating when the postponed item keeps coming to mind in a bothersome way. Another sure way to decide if this is actual procrastination or not, is to measure if the project gets bigger and more dreaded every time you think about it. As soon as you know it is one of those things, be kind to yourself and JUST DO IT!

I would give you some questions to answer, but you would probably just put them off until tomorrow anyway. Go have some fun instead!

RELEASE LETTERS

Writing a release letter is a marvelous way to get rid of the emotional garbage that all of us carry with us at one time or another. If you have anything that you are tired of lugging around, this is a great tool to have in your kit. You may be angry with someone (including yourself). You may have fear or guilt about something or someone. You may be tired of grieving the loss of a loved one, or perhaps you are angry with God or the Universe for the misfortune in your life.

The following must be included in each and every letter:

1. You must use a clean piece of full-sized paper.

2. Start the letter appropriately with a salutation:

  ✦ Dear God

  ✦ Dear Mom or Dad (or any other person)

  ✦ Dear (your own name)

3. State the intent of your letter in the first paragraph:

  ✦ *I am writing this letter in order to release the guilt I feel about…*

  ✦ *I am writing to release the anger I have been feeling about…*

  ✦ *I am writing this letter to release my fear or…*

4. Use as many lines, paragraphs, or pages as it takes to let out your real feelings about the issue that you are releasing. You can cuss and swear or use whatever language you need to use in order to say what you need to say. This is a great opportunity so get it all out and remember that no one will ever read it.

5. When you are done, you must write the following line: *"I release this (fear, anger, hatred, etc.) to the Highest Good of all concerned. I thank you for the lesson, but now I am done with it."*

6. End the letter with your signature and a closing of your choosing. (No cuss words at this point please. If you still feel like you need to use them, then you have to go back and write some more in body of the letter.)

7. Put the letter in an envelope and address it appropriately.

8. BURN THE LETTER in a manner that is safe, but effective. This is an absolute MUST because to hang on to the letter is to hang on to the problem. Disposing of the envelope in the garbage is not good enough.

SABOTAGE

Have you ever been working on a project most enthusiastically only to have it all turn sour? If it has happened to me once, it has happened a thousand times! From the sound of that statement one would think that some mysterious force of the Universe came along and ruined all of my hard work and zapped all of the dreams attached to it. My believing that, would make me a victim and since that is not acceptable to me, I must take responsibility for it. Nine times out of ten, the failure of the project is a self-imposed and self-prophesied occurrence. That is what sabotage is all about.

The "project" does not have to be anything huge. It could be as large as writing a novel or as small as agreeing to meet someone somewhere at a designated time. Anything in between could involve doing poorly at a job interview on purpose; failing an exam that you could have aced; being late for work on the day of an important meeting; or getting laryngitis the night before a singing recital.

So why would any of us do something that would almost certainly assure us of failure? *Sabotage is the occurrence of anything that stops or slows down an intended result, and at very best, lessens the rewards that would have come about if the retarding action had not happened.* This is a most interesting topic and the investigating of it reveals much about a person's spiritual and emotional make-up.

I have been the Queen of Sabotage! I would find ways to make all of my endeavors fail and those ways always involved fear—fear of succeeding, fear of commitment, fear of backing myself into a claustrophobic corner, fear of being caught being inadequate. The fears were so huge that I felt as though I had no choice except to make myself fail before I even began. My plan worked—until I found myself doing work that has life-changing importance and value to me. What I found out is that "Fear is not an excuse to quit; it is a reason to keep going." Scary, but true!

Questions

1. Think and write about a time when you have sabotaged yourself. Go into as much detail as you can because by doing so you may get a clue as to why you would have done this to yourself. Is this an isolated event or is sabotage a trend for you?

2. What was the payoff for you as a result of this sabotage?

3. Why do you think that you would intentionally or unintentionally sabotage yourself?

4. Do you have anything on the go at this time—mentally, physically, emotionally, or spiritually—that could be in danger of going to ruin at your own hand? What could you do to stop the sabotage—again?

5. Describe a project that you successfully took to completion. How did you feel while you were doing it? How did you feel when you finished it? Why do you think you let this one become a finished product?

SELF-LOVE

How often have you heard the phrase, *"You can't love anyone else until you truly love yourself"*? Every time I hear that statement I patronizingly nod my head and say, "Well, I must really love myself! To prove it, look at *all* the people I love!" Then I remember the times I have said, "I love my husband (or my children or Mom or the grandkids or my dogs…) more than I love life itself!" In my adamant declaration of devotion to them, I have put them ahead of me and that cancels out all that I have said about loving myself. Of course, we should love other people—even love them deeply—but we have to be careful not to sacrifice ourselves in the process.

I went on for a long time pondering this whole concept and watching for breakthroughs, no matter how small. My 'light bulb' moment came about on a level that I had ignored for most of my life—my physical self. Perhaps it would be more accurate to say that it started there and then moved inward. I realized that for many years I had shown myself on a daily basis exactly how much I <u>really</u> cared about myself by doing or not doing the following things:

✦ I ate and really enjoyed fatty foods at all hours of the day or night.

✦ I ate sweets and desserts on a daily basis—the more decadent the better!

✦ I put on weight that not only covered up the real me, but also forced my heart to work harder.

✦ I smoked for many years even though my father died from emphysema.

✦ I did very little, if any, exercise.

✦ I put everyone's needs ahead of mine, and saved no time or energy for myself.

✦ I did a lot of negative self-talk and denied myself simple pleasures.

✦ I sabotaged myself every time I got close to realizing my purpose.

✦ I had trouble forgiving myself for wrongs that I had done in the past.

✦ I put myself down constantly.

✦ For many years, I denied my own wisdom, my own truths, and my own gifts.

✦ I would not say "No!" to anyone and then I resented him or her for asking.

✦ I cringed to hear criticism, thinking it would hurt me, but now I see it as a wonderful tool for growth. (To be honest, I still do not like it!)

✦ I used to negate every accomplishment I made, by downplaying it until it disappeared.

✦ I believed everything—positive or negative—that anyone had to say about me.

The list could go on and on. Each of these points has damaged me and if I were to give this much abuse to anyone else I claimed to love, that person would be gone in a flash.

So one day, as I was looking into the mirror, I gazed deep into the eyes that were looking back at me, and I felt such love that I started to cry. I had to sit down because my legs felt like they had turned to jelly. I cried a long time, all the while saying over and over again, "I love you, Marilyn. I love you, Marilyn." I felt more joy than I had ever felt before and I mean that literally. Since that day, I have changed many items on the above list. I finally know that this body is not ME, but it is lent to me as a place to live during this lifetime. IF I had rented a house and taken as little care of it as I used to take care of my body, I would have been evicted a long time ago. My head and heart feel clarity unknown to me before and while I am full of energy, I also feel a peacefulness not know to me before.

I have noticed that people around me have changed—funny how that happens! I feel more respected. I feel more love. I now accept more love. I need less approval from others because I now approve of myself more. I feel more capable of doing anything that I choose to do. I feel like the world is open to me and all I have to do is to choose what I want to do and how and when—not if—I want to do it.

Self-Love

1. List all the ways that you have shown love for yourself. (Use as many sheets of paper as it takes!)

2. State 15 ways in which you have not loved yourself. (Put a check mark beside the ones you are willing to change and then really think about the ones that you are not.)

3. What is the most loving thing that you can do for yourself?

4. Tell about something said to you in childhood that may have prompted the idea that it is not good to love yourself too much. (i.e. Selfish? Self-centered?)

5. WRITE YOURSELF A LOVE LETTER.

TRUST THE PROCESS

These are the magic words! Whenever I feel a little overwhelmed by the world around me, I whisper the words *"Trust the Process!"* over and over again until I can feel it down to my toes. When you think about it, there is a process to everything—a natural way that things unfold. This unfolding is not always the same in any given event, but it always makes sense. Just as there is a process to the making of a baby and to all other seasonal aspects of Nature, so is there sense to all aspects of our lives.

I am in my sixth decade of living, and now am I finding out what my purpose is all about. I have wondered and wished and even lamented through the years why everyone else seemed to be doing what he or she liked, but nothing pleased me for long. I did not know that I was in the middle of a process of growth that I could not change and could not undo. Even after I first learned about the *trust the process* concept, I still had to wait, because I was not ready for the work for which I was being so lovingly groomed. When I was ready I was given the information and then it seemed so sensible, so perfectly planned, so right and, best of all, so easy!

When I originally wrote this piece in 2002 I was in the midst of a whirlwind of creative activity—mostly writing along with some public speaking. I absolutely felt the most alive when I was up on a stage speaking in front of people—the larger the crowd the better! Everyone who heard me speak praised me galore, but no one ever contacted me to speak to another group based on hearing me the first time. In fact, by mid 2003, my speaking engagements had dwindled down to nothing and so had the sale of my book *The Girl Behind the Closed Door*. I was feeling bad but in other ways, relieved, because I had been in quite a state of nervous energy and I was tired of it. In June of 2003 I got the inspiration (and I mean that in the most literal way) to move to Vancouver Island which we did in September of that same year.

When we got here to our new home I was so all consumed with decorating and getting settled that I did not take in the ramifications of our abrupt move until it was done. All of a sudden I sank into depression which resulted in me being medicinally treated for

Bipolar Disorder for the second time in my life. My creativity level went down to minus 100%. I did nothing but the mundane household tasks and felt relieved just to be doing something as simple as making the bed. When I was done with such a task, I would feel sad again. I missed my family (especially my mom) and friends in Edmonton so terribly much and I truly did not know what to do about it.

After about a year of just existing, I joined a couple of groups and started gardening in earnest for the first time in my life. I felt fulfilled for a while. I was convinced that I was meant to be here so that I could rest and just BE instead of living on the crazy inner roller coaster that I had been on for so very long. That thought held me steady for a couple of years. Then all of a sudden in February of 2007 the creative juices started flowing again. I was still on medication to balance my brain so I knew that this was not a manic high. In fact, it felt way better than that because it did not feel desperately urgent I resumed some writing that I had started years earlier and in an amazingly short time I was ready to get published and ended up having five books done instead of just one. Part way through the publishing process I got a little panicky because I felt I was in way over my head but then I remembered to *trust the process*. I had been brought here to do this work and I needed to have those years of balancing and rest before I would be ready. The phrase *trust the process* can also be stated as *"God brought me to it; God will take me through it."* I was in the midst of a pre-planned process and once I gave it that first nod of interest, I was all of a sudden in a tunnel of no return—I was too far in to turn back. So from there, I had no choice except to *trust the process*.

I have conceded that the path to public speaking in Edmonton had to go cold in order for me to get here to this beautiful place that has creativity built right into its air and water. From day-one this process has been in the making for me and so now I just have to face the fear, defy the doubt, and explode with the excitement of it all. I am in an amazing process and there is nothing left to do but trust it.

Questions

1. What is going on in your life right now that would be eased if you would trust the process?

2. Think back on an event that would have been so much easier to handle if you had trusted the process. Write about it.

3. If you are a worrier, how could using this concept improve your life?

ON BEING A VICTIM

Every good story involves a victim in danger and a hero who arrives in the nick of time to save him or her. Heroes are always handsome and heroines are always beautiful; all are seen as strong, powerful, and courageous. Kids try to imitate the heroic characters, but how often do you hear children fighting over who gets to be the victim? Not too often. That is because a victim looks quite undesirable when it is wearing someone else's skin and having someone else's name. However, many people do not realize that they, themselves, play that role every day of their lives and, in truth, they volunteer to do so. The same people would never willingly admit to being at the mercy of anyone or anything else and most would go into adamant denial if asked about it.

Commonly, victims feel that they have no choice in the matter. Things just happen to them. They blame their troubles on God, the state of the world, their own bad luck, their parents, or on the fact that life just sucks! When asked why they would volunteer to remain a victim the usual retort is, "Why would I want to have (this) happen to me? You must be out of your mind!" *(Usually it is not said that nicely!)*

Still others do not even realize that they are victims. They just think that life is tough and things are as they are! If a woman grows up watching her mother being put down and disrespected by the men in her life, then she thinks that is the normal state of affairs. She expects to be treated badly and so she usually is. Sadly, some very bad things can be accepted as 'normal' if they happen often enough over long periods of time. Only after seeing someone outside her family being treated kindly and respectfully by men, does she have any idea that she and the women before her have been victims (and unnecessarily so).

The trail *out* of Victimhood is one of the world's best-kept secrets and does not appear on any road maps. It is a wonderful route that I recommend to anyone who desires to improve his or her life. On this road you will never feel rushed and can drive at your own speed because of the very low traffic volume. However, what makes this roadway unique is that there are mandatory stops where you must fulfill a commitment before proceeding further. (There are turn-arounds in case you choose not to meet the necessary requirements.) These stops are very pleasant in their appearance, but they are sometimes painful to endure.

The first stop looks like a drive-in theatre from the 1950's. Each traveler is required to look at a movie depicting the memories that involved him or her while being a victim. The movie will put the person right back into the original pain of each incident while being lovingly protected through the whole viewing period. The price to continue down the road is *awareness and realization.* A few miles further on there is a stop that requires *acceptance* to advance. It is not possible to fool the man at the gate, because he knows when you are sincere. The road then goes on for many miles before coming to the biggest stop of all. This one has a huge parking lot, an hotel, and even a shopping center because many people stay here for a long time. There are traffic lights installed at the turn-around point because of the large volume of vehicles heading back to Victimhood. The toll to advance is *forgiveness* and that seems to be too big a toll for many people to pay. Those who do submit the payment are so empowered and so energized that the speed limit had to be lifted just to let them fly for a while. In spite of the newfound energy many motorists slow down to enjoy the beautiful scenery that now precedes them on the horizon. There is only one more stop to make and, again, there are motels because it takes a little time, but alas there are no crowds to content with. This stop requires you to take **responsibility** for your pain, and then **release** it to the man in the big tollbooth that marks the entranceway onto the Highway of Life. As you get onto that thoroughfare, you see a huge sign surrounded by tress, flowers, and a rainbow. This sign says:

> "Remember where you have been with love and kindness,
> because that will assure that you never have to return! Happy Motoring!"

Conversely, the road *going into* Victimhood is frantically busy at all hours of the day and night, and all that you can see for miles are concrete roadways and gray skies. People say that they do not plan to come to this place, but the chaos and the clamoring to get there suggest otherwise. As your travel agent today, I do not recommend this road at any time of the year. **Victimhood is not a nice place to visit and an even worse place to live.**

What are the payoffs?

THERE IS ALWAYS A PAYOFF!

Reflections On Being A Victim

1. Tell about an incident when you were treated in a way that you felt you did not deserve. Go into as much detail as possible. What were the payoffs?

2. Go into the incident described in question #1 and examine it using the steps on the road out of Victimhood.

- ✦ Awareness and realization of all the facts and the feelings involved.
- ✦ Acceptance that it happened for a good reason—whether you understand that reason or not. Realize that it may only make sense on the spiritual level. You just need to accept this possibility to let the healing begin.
- ✦ Forgive the person than perpetrated the action against you.
- ✦ Take Responsibility for the event and then let it go with love and kindness.

3. Have you ever made anyone else feel like a victim? Be honest with this and then write about anything that comes to mind. Be aware of it. Accept your actions. Ask for forgiveness (even if it is only from you). Take responsibility and release it with love. Use another sheet of paper if necessary.

4. What can you do to ensure that you will never be a victim again?

5. Can you go into a victim role and find the gifts? Take time on this because this is what brings the magic! *(Hint: "Some of the best gifts come wrapped in the ugliest wrapping paper.")*

WORDS THAT EXPRESS HOW WE FEEL

Every day of our lives someone asks us how we are. In fact, the words "How are you?" are inserted into greetings without any mind and often without any real interest in a truthful answer. When asked, do you ever tell the truth about the terrible day you are having? How would the other person react? I am sorry to say that most people do not really care how you are and are only asking because it is an automatic thing to say when two people meet.

Then there are the memories of being a child, especially if you were a child in the 1950's, when it was a common thing to be told, "A child should be seen, but not heard." I can remember feeling sad and being told that I had nothing to be sad about. I heard children who were crying being told, "If you don't stop crying, I will give you something to cry about." "You have no right to be sad, you ungrateful child." What about the oldest male child whose father has just died being told that he cannot cry because he is the man of the house now? I stopped seeing a doctor, who was also my therapist, when he said (after I had proclaimed how angry I was about something), "Judy, nice girls don't get angry."

We have been told for all of our lives how we should and should not feel. Is it any wonder that we are hard-pressed to know what we are feeling, let alone know *the right word to describe it?* We have been numbed by the belief that we have no right to feel or, if we do, we have no right to express it—at least not truthfully.

Have you ever been asked how you are and before you had a chance to reply, the person started talking about something else? My brother was once asked how he was and he truthfully replied that he had a migraine headache. Without missing a beat the person who asked him said, "Glad to hear it!" and then cheerfully went on to something else.

We all know that most people do not care when they inquire as to our well-being. Thus, we say such things in reply as "Fine," "Good," "OK," "Great," "So-so," "Pretty good," and so on. Have you noticed that not too many people ask you for an explanation about what those words mean when you use them to describe how you are?

I, however, do care how you are feeling when you undertake the lessons in this book (either alone or in a workshop). No matter how you are using this book just please remember to honor your feelings each day by choosing words that more adequately show how you are really feeling than "good" or "fine." In workshops, I like to do "feeling checks" and I will not accept those standard answers. It is time to put words onto your feelings and to be responsible for them. By that, I mean that sometimes you will be asked to explain what you have said.

On the following page I have listed all the descriptive words for feelings that I could think of. Please add to this list when you think of other words and share them with me, so that I can build an extensive reference for identifying our feelings. For those not in a workshop, I would be happy to hear from you by email if you have a word that should be on the list. (**marilynavient@shaw.ca**)

AFRAID	ENCUMBERED	JOYFUL	SAD
ANGRY	EXPOSED	JUDGED	SERENE
ASHAMED	EVIL	JUDGEMENTAL	SELFISH
ANXIOUS	EMPTY	JEALOUS	STUCK
ABUSED	EMPOWERED	LONELY	SECURE
ABANDONED	ENRAGED	LOVABLE	SAFE
ALONE	FEARFUL	LOVED	STRONG
ALIVE	FATIGUED	LOVING	TALENTED
BUBBLY	FRIENDLY	NEEDY	TRAPPED
BORED	FORGIVING	NERVOUS	USED
BRAVE	GIFTED	OVERWHELMED	UNDESERVING
CAPABLE	GENEROUS	OBLIVIOUS	UNIMPORTANT
CONTENTED	GUARDED	OPPRESSED	UNWORTHY
CLAUSTROPHOBIC	GUILTY	OVERBURDENED	UNLOVABLE
CHAOTIC	GRATEFUL	ORGANIZED	UNFRIENDLY
CENTERED	HAPPY	PEACEFUL	UNFORGIVING
COOPERATIVE	HELPLESS	PROUD	UNHEARD
CAUTIOUS	HOPEFUL	POSITIVE	UNBALANCED
CONFUSED	HOPELESSS	POWERFUL	UNLUCKY
DEPRESSED	HARMONIOUS	POWERLESS	UNKIND
DESERVING	INDIGNANT	PHONY	UNRELIABLE
DEPENDENT	INCAPABLE	PANICKY	VIOLATED
DEPENDABLE	INDEPENDENT	QUIET	VIOLENT
DECEIVED	INSIGNIFICANT	RECKLESS	VICTIMIZED
DECEPTIVE	INVISIBLE	RELIABLE	WEAK
DIGNIFIED	IMPATIENT	RESENTFUL	WEEPY
ELATED	IMPORTANT	RESERVED	
EXCITED	ISOLATED	SATISFIED	

Words That Express How We Feel

1. Looking back as far as you can remember, tell about a time when you were told to hide your feelings, mask your feelings, lie about your feelings, or get rid of your feelings.

2. Do you tell the truth about how you are when asked? Why or why not?

3. Tell about a time when someone inquired as to how you were feeling, and you got the impression that he or she really cared as opposed to just being polite. How did that make you feel and how did you handle it? How did the person indicate their sincerity?

4. Have you ever tried to be honest about your emotions only to be told that you do not really feel that way or that you have no reason and/or no right to do so?

5 EXERCISE: From now on, start being interested in how people really are feeling. Do not ask how someone is unless you REALLY want to know. What can you do to let the person know you really do care? If they do tell you something other than the usual reply, can you answer in such a way that they know they have been heard? Become aware of how many times you just automatically ask someone how they are instead of asking because you honestly care.

THE PRAYER OF ST. FRANCIS

God, make me an instrument of your peace.
Where there is hatred let me sow love.
Where there is injury let me sow pardon.
Where there is doubt, faith.
Where there is despair, hope.
Where there is darkness, light.
And where there is sadness, joy.

Grant that I may not seek so much to be consoled
As to console,
To be understood as to understand,
To be loved as to love.

For it is in giving that we receive,
It is in forgiving that we are forgiven,
And it is in dying that we are born to eternal life.

Other Books by Marilyn Avient:

"Free at Last
My Journey Into, Through, and Out of Depression"

"The Girl Behind the Closed Door"

Children's Books

"Judy's Rainbow"

"A Lesson for Neddy"

To ask questions about this workbook…
To inquire about the books listed above…
Or to book a speech or workshop
Contact Marilyn
at
marilynavient@shaw.ca
www.marilynavient.com

www.ingramcontent.com/pod-product-compliance
Ingram Content Group UK Ltd.
Pitfield, Milton Keynes, MK11 3LW, UK
UKHW051253180426
11947UKWH00020B/1703